FULL THROTTLE

INDY CARS

by
Sean McCollum

Consultant:
Donald C. Davidson
Historian
Indianapolis Motor Speedway
Indianapolis, Indiana

CAPSTONE PRESS
a capstone imprint

Books published by Capstone Press are manufactured with paper
containing at least 10 percent post-consumer waste.

Library of Congress Cataloging-in-Publication Data
McCollum, Sean.
    Indy cars / by Sean McCollum.
    p. cm. — (Edge books. Full throttle.)
    Summary: "Describes how Indy cars evolved into the highly advanced cars
they are today, as well as how teams prepare their cars for races and how races are
run" — Provided by publisher.
    Includes bibliographical references and index.
    ISBN 978-1-4296-3942-2 (lib. bdg.)
    1. Indy cars — Juvenile literature. I. Title.
TL236.M3727 2010
629.228 — dc22   2009022147

Editorial Credits
Carrie Braulick Sheely, editor; Tracy Davies, designer; Jo Miller, media researcher;
    Laura Manthe, production specialist

Photo Credits
AP Images, 9, 10; AP Images/Aynsley Floyd, 22; AP Images/Darron Cummings,
21; AP Images/Jeff Roberson, 20 (right); AP Images/Michael Conroy, 29; AP
Images/Michael DiNovo, 5; AP Images/Robert Azmitia, 27 (middle); AP Images/
Tom Strattman, 7; CORBIS/Paul Mounce, 20 (left); Courtesy of American
Honda Motor Co., Inc., 14; Getty Images Inc./Alvis Upitis, 12; Getty Images Inc./
Darrell Ingham, 17, 23; Getty Images Inc./Donald Miralle, 15; Getty Images Inc./
Panoramic Images, 27 (top); Getty Images Inc./Robert Laberge, 27 (bottom);
Newscom/MCT/Chicago Tribune/John Smierciak, 25; Shutterstock/CHEN WEI
SENG, 19; Shutterstock/Fedor Selivanov, 6 (top left); Shutterstock/Mike Brake, 6
(middle left); Shutterstock/PhotoD, 6 (bottom left); Shutterstock/Sergei Bachlakov,
cover; Shutterstock/Todd Taulman, 6 (top right), 8, 18

Artistic Effects
Dreamstime/In-finity; Dreamstime/Michaelkovachev; iStockphoto/Michael Irwin;
iStockphoto/Russell Tate; Shutterstock/Els Jooren; Shutterstock/Fedorov Oleksiy;
Shutterstock/jgl247; Shutterstock/Marilyn Volan; Shutterstock/Pocike

Table of Contents

HARD-CHARGING INDY CARS

In 2005, Ryan Briscoe was off to a good start in the Indy 300 race at Chicagoland Speedway. But on lap 20, Briscoe's car locked wheels with Alex Barron's car. Traveling at nearly 200 miles (322 kilometers) per hour, Briscoe's car launched into the air. It struck the safety barrier and fence. Then it ripped into pieces and exploded into flames.

Briscoe was very lucky. The car's strong **cockpit** held together. It skidded down the track with Briscoe still inside. Briscoe was badly bruised. He had slammed his head and broken a couple bones. Still, he walked away from the wreck.

Not only was Briscoe's car super-fast, but its tough design probably saved his life. By the next season, Briscoe was back in a new car, ready to race.

cockpit — the area of an Indy car where the driver sits

The rear of Briscoe's car smashed into the wall, while the nose got caught on the fencing.

Fast Fact: In 2008, Briscoe earned his first Indy Car Series win at the Milwaukee Mile race in Wisconsin.

Indy cars are the fastest cars in races that include laps. On these courses, they can roar to speeds of 230 miles (370 kilometers) per hour.

Indy Car

Which Race Car Is Which?

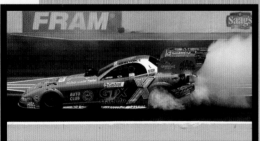

Formula One (F1) car
An F1 car looks very similar to an Indy car. Like an Indy car, it is open-wheeled. These cars have no fenders over the wheels. F1 cars race only on road courses, which include left and right turns. Indy cars compete on road courses as well as oval and other types of courses.

Dragster
A dragster races another car in a straight line down a short drag strip. Some dragsters reach almost 340 miles (547 kilometers) per hour.

Stock car
Stock cars are based on the models sold to the public. The most popular stock cars race in the NASCAR series. Indy cars and stock cars differ greatly in appearance, but they compete on many of the same courses.

Indy cars are easy to spot because of their unique shape. They ride low, standing a little more than 3 feet (.9 meter) off the track. Wings are attached to the cars' front and back ends. Drivers lean back in a cockpit. Only the driver's head peeks out. The car's design helps it cut through the air while keeping a tight grip on the track.

The Indianapolis 500

The Indianapolis 500, often called the Indy 500, is the world's most famous car race. About 300,000 fans attend the race at Indianapolis Motor Speedway every Memorial Day weekend. Millions more watch it on TV.

Thirty-three drivers battle it out for 500 miles (805 kilometers) during this classic race. The distance equals 200 laps around the track. A. J. Foyt, Al Unser Sr., and Rick Mears are tied for the most wins. Each has won the Indianapolis 500 four times.

(from left to right) Rick Mears, A. J. Foyt, and Al Unser Sr.

2

Indy Cars Through the Years

Like all race-car teams, Indy car crews are copycats. They quickly imitate other teams that win. Today, crews make small changes to cars, like changing the tire pressure. In the past, though, the changes were more noticeable. If you want proof, compare an Indy car photo from the early 1900s to a modern one. It will tell the tale of improvements through the years.

One thing has stayed the same through Indy racing history. Crews are under great pressure to improve car performance. For this reason, Indy cars have often been on the cutting edge of technology.

Modern Indy car bodies ride just above the track.

THE EARLY YEARS

The first cars in the Indianapolis 500 were wide and tall. Their big, boxy front ends held large engines. Top speeds were only around 80 miles (130 kilometers) per hour. But even back then, teams were trying to get an advantage. In the first Indianapolis 500 in 1911, Ray Harroun mounted a rearview mirror on his car. The ability to easily watch racers behind him helped Harroun clinch the win.

Like other cars in the 1911 Indianapolis 500, Ray Harroun's car was tall, wide, and long.

FASTER SPEEDS

In the 1920s, designers focused on engines, and Harry Miller built some of the best. Superchargers rammed air into the Miller engines for more power. By 1925, more than 70 percent of competing Indy cars had Miller engines.

Indy car bodies also slimmed down in the 1920s. The thinner bodies reduced **air resistance**. In 1925, Peter De Paolo became the first Indianapolis 500 winner to average more than 100 miles (161 kilometers) per hour for the entire race.

Gordon Johncock, Dan Gurney, and Mario Andretti (shown from left to right) won the best starting positions for the 1967 Indy 500 in their rear-engine cars.

NEW DESIGNS

In the 1950s, cars nicknamed "roadsters" roared onto the Indy car scene. With their rounded ends, roadsters looked like sub sandwiches. Powerful Offenhauser engines powered most roadsters. From 1947 to 1964, cars with Offenhauser engines won all the Indianapolis 500s.

A new car style ran roadsters off the track after 1965. In this design, the car's body was flatter and lower. The engine sat behind the driver instead of in front. The rear-engine design gave the cars better balance and handling around turns. In the 1965 Indianapolis 500, 27 out of 33 cars had rear engines. Cars with this design won the top four spots. By 1970, front-engine cars were a thing of the past.

air resistance — the force of air that pushes against and slows down moving objects

Fast Fact: Offenhauser engines were named for Fred Offenhauser. Fred had worked for Harry Miller. The Offenhauser engine was based on one of Miller's successful designs.

AERODYNAMICS AND DOWNFORCE

After the 1960s, designers paid more attention to **aerodynamic** car bodies. The easier a car sliced through the air, the faster it went and the less fuel it burned. Lower, more pointed cars became the norm.

There was a problem, though. The cars became harder to control as they topped 150 miles (241 kilometers) per hour. They tended to lift, causing a dangerous loss of grip on the track.

The solution? Wings. Usually, wings lift objects into the air, like aircraft. But wings on Indy cars were mounted upside down on the front and rear ends. As the air rushed over them, they pushed the cars down onto the track instead. This effect is called downforce. It gave drivers more control of their cars at high speeds.

Wings on Indy cars allowed drivers to take corners at higher speeds.

Wings had a powerful impact. They were first allowed in the Indianapolis 500 in 1971. The next year wings were back and they were bigger. They helped Bobby Unser earn the **pole position** with a speed of nearly 196 miles (315 kilometers) per hour. That was 17 miles (27 kilometers) per hour faster than the top qualifying speed the year before. It was the largest one-year speed increase in the race's history! By the late 1970s, continuing design improvements let drivers regularly top 200 miles (322 kilometers) per hour.

aerodynamic — designed to reduce air resistance

pole position — the inside starting position in the first row; the spot is usually earned by having the fastest qualifying time.

Fast Fact: Indy cars produce so much downforce that they could race on an upside-down track.

3

MARVELS OF MODERN DESIGN

Today's Indy cars are wonders of race-car engineering. High-tech equipment gives crews more control than ever. Car engines crank out more than 600 horsepower. At the same time, the specially designed chassis provides stability.

THE ENGINE

All Indy cars began using the Honda Indy V-8 engine in 2006. The engine's eight **cylinders** are set in a "V" shape. This power plant cranks out about 650 horsepower. That's three to four times the power of most passenger cars. The Honda V-8 is tough and dependable. It can handle up to 1,400 miles (2,253 kilometers) of racing before needing to be rebuilt. Unlike some past Indy engines, the Honda V-8 doesn't use a supercharger or other device to bring in more air.

cylinder – one of the hollow cylindrical-shaped chambers inside an engine in which fuel burns

To form the "V" shape of the engine, four cylinders are placed on each side.

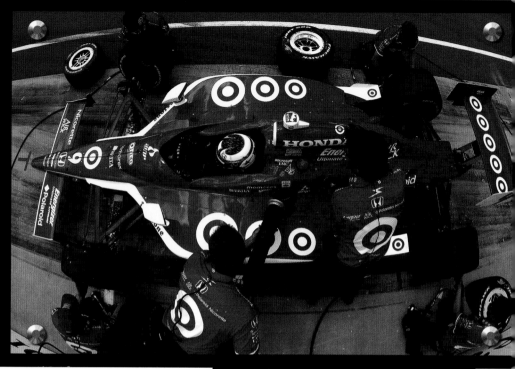

An Indy car's fuel tank holds 22 gallons (83 liters) of fuel-grade ethanol.

Indy
Goes Green

Indy cars switched from methanol to fuel-grade ethanol for the 2007 season. The Indy Car Series became the first series in motorsports to compete on a renewable fuel. Ethanol is renewable because it is made from corn, which can be replaced quickly.

Indy cars use the same chassis, too. It is made by Dallara, an Italian company. The chassis is monocoque (MAH-nuh-coke), which means "single shell." This design combines a car's body with the frame, making the car stronger and lighter. The smooth outer shell of the chassis is made of **carbon fiber**. Under this shell is an aluminum core that looks like honeycomb. The core helps absorb the impact in case of a crash.

To give drivers more control, air inlets called venturi tunnels are built under the chassis **sidepods**. These tunnels create an area of low pressure between the chassis and the track. The low pressure creates suction. Also called "ground effect," the suction helps hold the cars to the track.

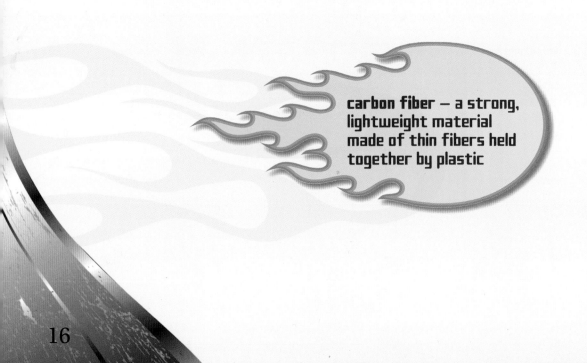

carbon fiber – a strong, lightweight material made of thin fibers held together by plastic

Helio Castroneves speeds down the track at Kansas Speedway on April 26, 2009.

sidepod — the bodywork on the left and right sides of an Indy car; sidepods cover the car's radiator, engine control unit, and oil cooler.

INDY CARS AT A GLANCE

Top speed	about 230 miles (370 kilometers) per hour
Engine	3.5-liter V-8
Horsepower	about 650
Gearbox	six-speed paddle shift
Fuel Capacity and Type of Fuel	22 gallons (83 liters) of fuel-grade ethanol
Tires	grooved racing slicks
Wheelbase (length from front wheel to back wheel)	about 122 inches (310 centimeters)
Height	about 38 inches (97 centimeters)
Width	77.5-78.5 inches (197-199 centimeters)
Weight	at least 1,575 pounds (714 kilograms) for oval courses; 1,640 pounds (744 kilograms) for road courses

Vitor Meira practices for the 2008 Indy 500.

Indy Cars vs. F1 Cars

F1 cars are the closest cousins of Indy cars. The cars look alike because they are both open-wheeled. But Indy cars can travel about 5 miles (8 kilometers) per hour faster. Also, F1 cars use unleaded gasoline and have a different type of transmission.

F1 Car

Fast Fact: The advanced Indy car design comes with a high price tag. An Indy car chassis costs about $309,000. Leasing the Honda V-8 engine costs about $1,000,000 a year. And the bill for tires? About $250,000 per season for each car.

Dozens of computer sensors are built into an Indy car's engine, chassis, and other parts. They constantly gather information such as the car's oil temperature and fuel pressure. The sensors automatically send reports to computers in the pit area.

The feedback from the sensors helps pit crews make smart, quick changes to cars. For example, sensors may show that the driver needs to brake too hard in the turns. At the next pit stop, the team might adjust the car's wings to create more downforce.

Large screens in the pit area display feedback from a car's computers.

steering wheel controls

RACING SLICKS

Indy car tires are called slicks. During a race, the slicks heat up to more than 200 degrees Fahrenheit (93 degrees Celsius) — almost hot enough to boil water! The hot rubber becomes sticky to give the car extra **traction**.

Firestone supplies tires to Indy race teams. The company delivers a certain number of slicks to each team before a race. This supply must last through practice, **qualifying laps**, and the race. The number of tires depends on the race's length. For the Indianapolis 500, most teams get 35 sets of four slicks per car.

Pit crews keep tires organized so they are ready on a moment's notice.

qualifying lap — a lap driven around the track to determine a driver's starting position for the race

traction — the grip of a car's tires on the ground

SAFETY FEATURES

Driving at 230 miles (370 kilometers) per hour is never entirely safe. But race officials work tirelessly to make it as safe as possible. Safety features prove themselves in crashes like Ryan Briscoe's in 2005.

An Indy car's strong chassis is one of its best safety features. Even though smaller pieces may break off in a crash, the chassis is built to hold together.

A car's Suspension Wheel/Wing Energy Management System (SWEMS) is made up of restraints. The restraints are made of a strong material called zylon. They help keep the wheels and wings attached in case of a wreck. Otherwise, these parts could fly off and hit other cars or fans.

Indy cars also have an attenuator on the back end. It supports the rear wing and helps absorb the force of a rear-end crash.

Ryan Briscoe's cockpit skidded down the track before stopping near the grassy infield.

Safety equipment is not just a part of the cars. A driver wears a helmet, a HANS (Head and Neck Support) device, and a fire-resistant suit. Safety harnesses strap drivers into their seats.

Drivers are in full safety gear every time they step into the cockpit.

23

In 2008, Helio Castroneves was starting in 28th place for the Indy 300 at Chicagoland Speedway. That was the last starting position. But the Indy star refused to stay there. By lap three he had moved up to 18th place. By lap 39 he had weaved his way into the top 10. And by lap 78 he was fighting for the lead.

On the last lap, he was side by side and nose to nose with Scott Dixon. The checkered flag waved.

Who won? At first, race officials gave Dixon the victory. Then they checked the finish-line photo. Castroneves had nipped Dixon by less than 13 inches (33 centimeters) and 0.0033 seconds. It was the second closest finish in Indy car history.

Indy car races are filled with heart-pounding moments. As the season goes along, the rivalry between teams heats up. They are all after one thing — enough points to claim the championship.

Dixon (car #9) and Castroneves were side by side just a few hundred yards from the finish line.

Fast Fact: The closest Indy car finish happened in 2002. Sam Hornish Jr. edged out Al Unser Jr. by 0.0024 seconds at Chicagoland Speedway.

The Indy Racing League (IRL) oversees all Indy car races and teams. It sets the car design requirements and makes racing rules. The Indy Car Series season stretches from spring to fall. It usually includes 15 to 19 races.

A few races are run on road courses like Watkins Glen International. This New York track features 11 turns on its 3.37-mile (5.4-kilometer) layout. Elsewhere, cities map out Indy races on their streets. These races include the Streets of Long Beach in California and the Streets of Toronto in Ontario, Canada. Road and street courses require a lot of hard braking and steering wheel wrestling to make hairpin turns.

Most Indy car races, though, are held on large ovals. The most famous of these tracks is the Indianapolis Motor Speedway. Average speeds on ovals are often double the speeds on road courses because drivers make fewer turns.

Drivers in the Indy Car Series earn points depending on how they finish a race. First place earns 50 points, second earns 40, and third picks up 35 points. Drivers in lower placings receive fewer points. The driver with the most points at the end of the season earns the championship title.

*oval track,
Indianapolis
Motor
Speedway*

*street course,
St. Petersburg,
Florida*

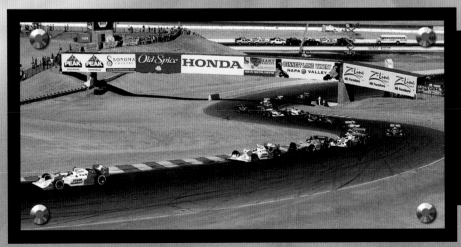

*road course,
Infineon
Raceway*

27

Indy car teams usually roll into town two to three days before a race. They take a day to prepare their cars and practice on the track. They adjust the car's setup to get it just right for that course.

Teams also go through a series of qualifying events. First officials inspect the cars to make sure they meet all the requirements. Then drivers run qualifying laps. The number of qualifying laps drivers do depends on the course. A driver's highest average lap speed determines the starting race position.

The Perfect Pit Stop

Every second counts once an Indy car pulls into the pit box during a race. The pit crew instantly springs into action. The "perfect" pit stop takes eight seconds.

0.0 seconds	Car pulls into pit box. Six pit crew members jump over the wall.
0.5 seconds	The air jack raises the car and the fueler connects the fuel hose.
2.0 seconds	Four tire changers remove the racing slicks.
5.0 seconds	New wheels are bolted into place.
6.0 seconds	The air jack drops the car to the ground and the crew makes wing adjustments.
7.0 seconds	The fueler finishes filling the car's 22-gallon (83-liter) fuel tank.
8.0 seconds	The Indy car leaves the pit box with a push from the crew.

RACING INTO THE FUTURE

Today's top Indy car drivers include Scott Dixon, Helio Castroneves, and Dario Franchitti. Drivers combine physical ability with mental toughness. They must have tiger-like reflexes to make a pass in tight traffic. At the same time, they must know when to back off to save fuel and avoid trouble. "It's a demanding sport," driver Bruno Junqueira said in an interview. "The guy that's more prepared physically wins."

Combining powerful cars with smart, gutsy drivers adds up to great Indy car racing. The sport and its screaming machines have a long, rich history that shows no signs of slowing down.

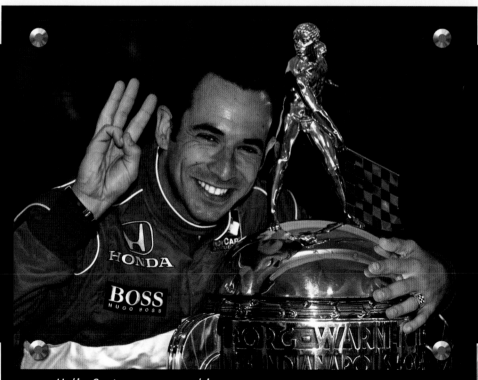

Helio Castroneves won his third Indy 500 in 2009.

GLOSSARY

aerodynamic (ayr-oh-dy-NA-mik) — designed to reduce air resistance

air resistance (AYR ri-ZIS-tuhns) — the force of air that pushes against and slows down moving objects

carbon fiber (KAHR-buhn FY-buhr) — a lightweight material made of strong, thin fibers held together by plastic

chassis (CHA-see) — the main framework of a vehicle to which the other parts are fixed

cockpit (KOK-pit) — the area of an Indy car where the driver sits

cylinder (SI-luhn-duhr) — one of the hollow cylindrical-shaped chambers inside an engine; fuel burns in the cylinders to create power.

downforce (DOUN-fors) — the downward air pressure that helps a race car grip the track

horsepower (HORSS-pou-ur) — a unit for measuring an engine's power

pole position (POHL puh-ZISH-uhn) — the inside spot in the front row of cars at the start of a race; drivers earn the pole position by having the best qualifying lap time.

qualifying lap (KWAHL-uh-fye-ing LAP) — a lap driven around a track to determine a driver's starting position for a race

setup (SEHT-uhp) — the fine-tuning and positioning of a race car's brakes, suspension, and other systems

sidepod (SYD-pod) — the bodywork on the left and right sides of an Indy car chassis

traction (TRAK-shuhn) — the grip of a car's tires on the ground

Read More

Brennan, Kristine. *Danica Patrick.* Modern Role Models. Philadelphia: Mason Crest, 2009.

McCollum, Sean. *Racecars: the Ins and Outs of Stock Cars, Dragsters, and Open-Wheelers.* RPM. Mankato, Minn.: Capstone Press, 2010.

Piehl, Janet. *Indy Race Cars.* Motor Mania. Minneapolis: Lerner, 2007.

Tieck, Sarah. *Indy Cars.* Amazing Vehicles. Edina, Minn.: ABDO, 2009.

Internet Sites

FactHound offers a safe, fun way to find Internet sites related to this book. All of the sites on FactHound have been researched by our staff.

Here's all you do:

Visit *www.facthound.com*

FactHound will fetch the best sites for you!

Index